MW00513129

DARRIN

LAUNᴄ.. ..

The Ultimate Guide to Product Launching, Learn All the Best Tactics and Useful Tools on How to Create and Launch Your Own Product Line

Descrierea CIP a Bibliotecii Naţionale a României
DARRIN SOMMER
LAUNCH IT. The Ultimate Guide to Product Launching, Learn All the Best Tactics and Useful Tools on How to Create and Launch Your Own Product Line / Darrin Sommer – Bucharest: Editura My Ebook, 2021
ISBN

DARRIN SOMMER

LAUNCH IT

The Ultimate Guide to Product Launching, Learn
All the Best Tactics and Useful Tools on How to
Create and Launch Your Own Product Line

My Ebook Publishing House
Bucharest, 2021

TABLE OF CONTENTS

INTRODUCTION

A product launch is the most powerful way to build a lot of excitement and anticipation for a product, as well as to guarantee a huge explosion of sales where otherwise you might have seen a slow trickle at best. When launching a product, you are creating a buzz and a build-up around your item and that will not only ensure that you gain maximum conversions when you first release your ebook, course or physical product; it will also help you to keep generating more and more income over time. It will help you to recruit affiliates, create fans and strengthen your brand. With a strong start, you can create momentum for your product that ensures it continues to grow as word of mouth spreads and the news travels. Your product launch will become an unstoppable force...

Think about the way that big brands launch vs the way that most internet marketers launch. Many of us will simply quietly release an ebook or a course on our website and *hope* that sales gravitate toward it. One day a link appears on our website to 'Buy My Book!' and pretty much everyone just keeps on web surfing right past it.

Conversely, think about the way that a company like Apple or like Microsoft will launch a product. It normally starts with rumours, leaks and whispers. Apparently Apple has a new product in the works. Apparently it's going to be the biggest and most exciting product they've released *yet*.

Apparently it's going to change the world!

Then a date is placed for the announcement. Normally, this will take place at an event run by the company where they'll be talking on stage. People count down the days while news outlets speculate. And when that date comes, people will tune in to watch all around the world: often going as far as to stay up late to watch their favorite brand do their thing.

The product is then displayed in a stunning, surprising and elegant manner. People still quote Steve Jobs' famous 'One more thing...' That wasn't just a product launch, it was a moment in history and popular culture.

And during these talks, that's also when the product launch itself is announced. And that's when people get even *more* excited. That's when the anticipation builds up to fever pitch.

8

They've seen it, they've heard about it, they've been imagining it for years... and now they must have it!

Imagine if you launched like that. Imagine if you could get that kind of buzz going for your product!

What You Will Learn

In this book, that's exactly what you're going to learn. Now, of course you're never going to launch quite as big as Apple. Apple is one of the biggest companies in the world, it has a hugely loyal fan base and it has the eyes and ears of the world's media. If you are a small internet marketer then you *just* don't have that same kind of influence or clout.

But that's not to say that you can't still learn from the company. And it's not to say that you can't still have a big impact when you eventually do launch.

In this ultimate guide to launching a product, you'll learn how you can make a massive splash whether you have a gigantic brand or you're one guy working out of a dorm room. You'll learn how to leverage and make full use of what you *do* have and you'll see how to get people talking, how to get people excited and how to grow your audience and potential market as the date of your launch draws closer.

If you have a mailing list of 100 people, then a good launch can be the difference between 30% of those readers making a purchase and 85% making a purchase. What's more, if you do it right, you can easily expect to see that list double or triple in size as you draw closer to your launch.

To do all this, you will learn:

- How to choose the perfect product to launch
- How to make a product sound desirable before it is even complete
- How to use your launch to build authority and influence
- How to develop your product during the lead up to your launch
- The best tools to use to spread the word and get people talking
- How to work with top influencers and marketers to build massively more excitement
- How to make sure your launch doesn't fall flat
- How early to start promoting your launch
- How to use the launch to run special offers and deals
- How to know the optimum time to launch
- How to create a perfect product

- How to work with products that are not your own...

- How to build a sales page so your product keeps growing

- How to handle the post-launch phase and use one successful product to launch another

Once you develop this often overlooked skill, you'll be able to massively increase the number of sales for *any* product, build more authority and trust and generally take your marketing business to the next level.

CHAPTER 1

THE POWER OF THE PERFECT LAUNCH

The launch is often one of the last things that creators and marketers think about when creating their product. They spend ages thinking about the nature of the product itself (rightly so), they think about their basic marketing strategies (again, this is a good idea) and they think about things like pricing, funding etc.

But who spends a considerable amount of time thinking about the launch and the build-up to the launch?

The truth is that many marketers simply aren't fully aware of just how important this is. All too many marketers think of their launch as being the boring and straightforward bit that comes once they've done all of the important parts. But this is a massive mistake...

Why Your Launch is *Hugely* Important

We already talking in the introduction a little about why it is so important to have a big product launch. To recap, this allows you to build more excitement and buzz around your product, ensuring that the people who visit your website regularly don't miss the fact that you've launched your product and making it seem that much more important and exciting to them.

The simple fact that someone has to wait for a product is enough to ensure that it is going to seem more important, more exciting and more newsworthy. The fact that you're dedicating so much time to it, demonstrates that this isn't just another boring ebook or course that you created as a second thought. It becomes an exciting *event* and that means that people are instantly going to want to get involved.

More to the point, this gives your product more time to become desirable in the minds of your audience. As soon as your audience *can't have* the product that you're promoting, you're going to find that they want it *considerably* more. As soon as your audience is made to wait, they're going to build up the product in their minds and make it seem a thousand times more exciting.

If you time this just right, then you'll have built your audience up to a fever pitch by the time your product actually becomes available.

With this launch, you can ensure that the moment your product goes live, it will enjoy a sudden and very powerful influx of orders. The excitement of your launch and build-up will even help to color the impressions that your audience have of the product - it will seem ten times better simply because your audience was so excited about it before they got their hands on it!

And that initial surge is going to help sales going forward too. That initial surge will be enough to get people talking about your product - you can expect reviews to start popping up and discussions in forums. What's more, is that depending on your distribution platform, that initial surge can help to get you more prominence.

For instance, if you have a strong launch on Amazon, then it's going to take your product to the top of the search results for that niche, helping you to gain *even more* sales. And this will be helped strongly by a sudden injection of strong reviews.

Meanwhile, if you are promoting your product through an affiliate network like JVZoo or ClickBank (where you can find marketers to help you sell your books), then you're going to find that the great time:sales ratio will help you attract even more marketers to your cause.

It is absolutely no exaggeration to say that the way you handle your launch can make or break your chances of having a highly successful product on your hands.

More Benefits of a Product Launch

But there are more reasons that your product launch and the build-up to it are so important.

For starters, creating a product launch gives you the opportunity to create a dialogue between yourself and the people you are selling to. This then means that you can ask them for feedback and ideas and thereby tailor the product for the exact audience that you're selling it to.

Think about it: this is a foolproof strategy as you are simply asking your buyers what they want and then creating that exact product!

A great way to do this is by creating a beta test for your product. This lets people sign up to try out an unfinished version of your product and provide feedback. This has the benefit of not only allowing you to test out your concept and see if it is getting the desired result but also to build even more excitement for what you're selling! It's no coincidence that more and more platforms online are introducing beta tests as a common option for creators and buyers: such as the gaming platform 'Steam' and its 'early access' option.

Likewise, you can also benefit from a product launch by inviting pre-orders. When you invite pre-orders you are not only improving your cashflow (this can even be used as a way to fund the creation of the project!) but also verifying your market. This means you'll be able to test the reception for your product before you actually go live - thereby ensuring that you don't spend years and years on a highly expensive product that only sells two units.

If you're collecting pre-orders and you're allowing people to sign up, then you can potentially breakeven *even before* you have released your product. And this will be enough for you to consider putting in more features etc.

In fact, you can even borrow from Kickstarter (something we'll be looking at more in a moment) and introduce 'stretch goals' and the like to encourage more sales still wherever possible.

Then there's the fact that a launch can instantly create authority for you, your brand and the product itself. As we mentioned, the perception is that only a very exciting and important product would have that much buzz around it - and especially if you have internet marketers involved so that it isn't just you creating buzz for your own item.

Finally, creating a big product launch is a great opportunity to run special offers, deals and other campaigns that can only further enhance your sales. It's common to give discounts to people who preorder for example, but what about giving money off for the first few sales? This is a great way to create more urgency surrounding your product and thereby invite even more sales. Or about building even more excitement by giving people money off for referring a friend? Another option is to add extra features to your product or to alter the price if you can generate a certain number of likes for your Facebook page etc.

Creating a launch isn't *just* a way to go big on your product then, it's also a great opportunity to introduce many other exciting strategies and to take full advantage of the excitement that you're creating.

CHAPTER 2

WHAT TO LAUNCH? TYPES OF PRODUCTS THAT LEND THEMSELVES TO BUILDING BUZZ

Now you know why it's so important to have a big launch for your product, you're probably eager to get out there and launch something!

The next question then, is precisely what you're going to launch. What types of products lend themselves to a big build-Up? What type of products can become an event?

The short answer to this question is: anything. You can sell digital products, physical products, informational products, services... pretty much *anything* and add a launch.

This is the first takeaway to learn from this book in fact. If you are running a writing service or a web design service, then it can sometimes pay to change the way you think about that service and to approach it more as you might a product. This is sometimes referred to as 'productizing' a service. And in this case, you could think about the kind of new service-product you could launch. How about a '2 For 1' package that will be coming in limited supply next month? Message your client list and this can potentially give them time to prepare their budget for some smart bulk-orders.

Likewise, the more ambitious internet marketers can use a product launch as a way to sell a physical item. You'd be surprised just how easy it is to start selling physical products these days and you actually have *many* different options: whether you intend on selling a product that you had very little involvement in via a dropshipping company (essentially a company that lets you act as though it is your product but that handles manufacturing and fulfilment) or whether you actually want to create something from scratch by using a manufacturer and ordering a MOQ (Minimum Order Quantity).

But for most people reading this, launching a product is going to mean launching a digital product to begin with...

Types of Digital Product to Launch

Of course, there are lots of obvious advantages to selling a digital product. This is a product that has zero overheads and that you can sell completely for free, while keeping 100% of the profits. At the same time, it requires no upfront investment either, doesn't need any storage and doesn't even require fulfilment. This is also the easiest type of product when it comes to getting other marketers to help and setting up an affiliate scheme.

When it comes to the types of digital product you can launch, there are a few common options. Some of the best though include:

- Video course
- Membership site
- Ebook
- Coaching
- Software or app

Each of these are things that you can create using relatively standard tools and no special skills and from there, you'll be able to start selling and making profit right away.

These are largely informational products. That means that what you're selling really is the information that the ebook or course contains and the precise format is really nothing more than the means of delivery.

How to Ensure Your Product Builds Buzz

Whatever you decide to sell, the most important thing to consider from our perspective at this point, is how you're going to make that product seem exciting and appealing. We're going to be spending the rest of this ebook trying to get people excited for the product that we've created and that is partly going to come down to the specific marketing techniques we use to get people talking and to make the product sound amazing.

But what's just as important, is to think about the way that the product is going to *lend* itself to that marketing to begin with.

Case in point: if you are making an ebook about cooking, then that might sell very well. It has a very clear niche and solves a very clear problem.

But now if you try and build *buzz* for that product you might struggle. That's not to say that the product isn't good, just that it isn't the kind of thing that necessarily lends itself to a big launch.

The same goes for a product like a calendar app. Or a product like a t-shirt.

The problem is that these products don't have that inherent excitement or interest that will make people get truly excited.

Here's the simple thing to know when choosing the type of product to use for a big launch: products that cost more, are generally more exciting for the customers. That might sound odd, seeing as you'd think that people would be more excited by a great deal. But the fact of the matter is that a product that is a bit more expensive and a bit more luxury is a product that *needs* forethought, that *needs* build up and that is worthy of the excitement and anticipation.

Think about it this way: what do you think about more? What do you get more excited about in the build-up to? Buying a t-shirt, or buying a new suit? The answer is obvious.

But of course the cost of that item has to be reflected in the quality and the inherent excitement. So then the next question is: how do you make a digital product like an ebook into something that is highly exciting and that people would be willing to potentially pay a lot of money for?

The big thing to focus on here, is what is known as the 'value proposition', which we can loosely translate as 'the dream'.

In other words, you have to know what dream it is your selling. When you sell information, what you are *really* selling is a means to an end. What will your audience do with that information? What is it that makes them want that information so badly in the first place?

So for example, if you are selling a book about fitness, then your information will probably relate mostly to diets, to exercises and to health. What does an audience want with such information?

Simple: they want to be fitter and healthier. And why do they want to be fitter and healthier? Most likely to improve their confidence, to improve their athletic prowess, so they'll feel healthier in the mornings and maybe so they'll improve their sex lives.

Now *that* is something that you can sell and that people can get excited for.

Likewise, if you are selling a book about making money, then you can sell the dream of feeling powerful and successful, of wearing a smart suit, of being able to travel... You can get the audience to picture having their own boat, their own holiday home and a big, sprawling internet empire.

These are things that can build excitement!

The other element to think about when choosing what kind of product to create, is the element of mystery and excitement. That is to say, that the very best products when it comes to

24

launching, are going to be those that have some 'new' element about them, or some mysterious element. Likewise, they should be somehow desirable.

This is why the iPhone launches always work so well. The products are hugely exciting for fans because they have the element of something new and unusual about them. They're shrouded in mystery until the moment of their unveiling and once they *are* unveiled, they'll be celebrated for their new features and things that people just haven't seen before.

Leading up to the announcement, people will wonder how the product is going to function, what new features it will have and how it is going to be different from last year. The most disappointing launches are those where the iPhones are pretty much the same as last year and this is what has led many people to insinuate that perhaps Apple has lost its 'edge' without Steve Jobs.

During the launch itself, it will be common for the person presenting the gadget to use a lot of emotive words and words that make the device seem more desirable. Those include words like 'feel' and 'imagine'. 'Beautiful', 'incredible to hold', 'premium', 'luxury', 'heavy in the hand'...

So how can we take these ideas and get them to work for our digital products? How can you make something intangible like an ebook seem more premium, more exciting and more mysterious?

The first tip is to try and give your book a new edge. That means it shouldn't just be 'yet another book on how to lose weight'.

Instead, this is 'the game-changing program that is transforming lives behind the scenes'. It's a 'totally new approach to training that will bring unheard of results'.

Likewise, it's not just a book on making money but rather a 'complete and comprehensive guide to the world of digital marketing' or 'a new system for generating huge money while you sleep'.

It has to be different, whether that means it's just better, or whether that means it is going to be unique in terms of its approach.

The other tip is to dress up your product and make it more exciting and interesting that way. So this time, it's not just a matter of selling an ebook but maybe filling that ebook with beautiful, stunning art. Maybe it means giving away a free video course as well, a t-shirt, or access to a membership area on your site. Maybe it means they get a physical copy of the book, or maybe it means that the book is simply so comprehensive as to be the ultimate guide.

Perhaps if you've ever played computer games, you will remember how exciting it was to get a game that came with a detailed instruction manual, a metal tin, a collectible figurine. Then you'd get a map you could pull out to help you find your way around the game world, a guide to the shortcuts and hotkeys you could use to change weapon, or to exert various effects...

These sorts of features make a product much more exciting and desirable, even though they don't add much to the core experience. The key is to include things that people can *imagine* holding and owning. Things that will make your product stand out from the crowd, feel 'ultimate' somehow. and generally just be something that's worth getting excited about.

Some More Tips for Choosing a Niche

We're getting ahead of ourselves a little here though, as we of course need to choose a niche first. Your aim is going to be to select a niche that is popular and easy to market, with that great 'value proposition'. At the same time though, think about the assets and skills available to you.

It is *always* a good idea to pick a niche that you know well for instance, especially if you plan on handling the product creation yourself. At the same time, it is also always a good idea to choose a niche that you have good connections and contacts in already.

In other words, if you happen to be good friends with someone who owns a massive website, then it's going to make a lot of sense for you to create a product in that niche. This is something we'll look at shortly in more detail.

CHAPTER 3

CREATING YOUR PRODUCT

With the basic idea of your product in mind, you can now start to actually create it and build it.

Do you need to have your product complete before you enter the pre-launch phase? Not at all - and especially not if, as we have suggested, you plan on using this phase to generate ideas and advice and possibly even to rack up some funding to help make the product a reality.

But you should at least have some of it completed before you start marketing. This will help you to create a more authentic marketing campaign (so that your marketing reflects the final product), it will give you more materials to use (such as screenshots etc.) and it will avoid any unfortunate delays or other issues.

Planning Your Product

Once you have chosen the type of product you want to create, you next need to go about creating a skeleton outline for it. This is going to come in handy as you work through the materials to ensure that you aren't missing anything crucial. At the same time though, you're also going to find that this comes in very handy should you outsource your creation - having a basic outline will ensure that you and your creator are on the same page and help them to know precisely what it is you want to communicate through your product.

If it's an ebook then, you need to start by breaking down what you're going to teach into chapters. Likewise, for a course you'll need to come up with some basic modules or lessons. Choose too the format (email, video, document etc.) and the delivery.

It's also a good idea to spend some time budgeting and working out how long this is all going to take. One of the easiest ways for your plans to get derailed, is to set out to write a killer ebook but then never actually get past chapter 5! Make sure you know how long you need to work on your book and set yourself some units of time when you can work on it. Maybe that means an hour a week, or maybe two hours a day!

If you're going to outsource the creation, then you need to think about the cost of writing or videography and then calculate how much you're looking at in total.

Getting Down to It

The precise methods you use to create your product are going to vary depending on the type of product you ultimately choose to make. We can't go every single possibility in detail here but we can certainly provide a brief outline for each of the major options...

Ebook

Creating an ebook is perhaps one of the easiest options for product creators. This requires no specialist software and no specialist skills - as long as you can write good English and you have a copy of Microsoft Word (or Google Docs/Open Office), then you can simply set about writing your own ebook. Remember to include images and to employ some attractive layout options. This is where using Word makes a little more sense in particular, as it will allow you to easily insert a Table of Contents, page numbers, background images etc.

A very basic length for an ebook is 10,000. But remember: this is supposed to be an exciting and new idea, so you want to ensure that the final product is something special. An 'ultimate' ebook can be anywhere from 12,000 words to 100,000. Remember, a typical 'technical' book that is a hard copy is going to be around 100,000 words, so you need to aim big if you're going to make your book something really special. At the same time as word count, think hard about the layout.

Make sure that the information you're providing is exciting and new. It is not good enough to research the topic and then write a generic book on that subject matter: you need to choose a topic that you know well and this is what will then give you the ability to think outside the box and to create something really unique and interesting.

When you're done, make sure that you save the file in .PDF format, which will mean that people who download it can zoom in and won't be able to edit the document. Another option is to upload your book to Kindle (https://kdp.amazon.com/), which you can do very easily with no need to change the format of the book and which is actually free as well!

Video Course

If you're creating a video course then you have two options: one is to create a tutorial or slideshow course, in which case you won't need to be physically present in your own videos. The other is to create a 'talking head' course, or to create a video product.

Creating a video course that you are not in is relatively simple. If you're going to be making a video tutorial showing people how to do various things on-screen, then you can accomplish this using software like ScreenFlow for Mac (https://screenflow.en.softonic.com/mac) or like Camtasia (http://go.softwarecasa.com/camtasia/) for PC.

On the other hand, another way to go about doing this is to simply create a slideshow and then talk over the top of it. That slideshow can include ideas, tips and information and all you need to do is to record a vocal track and edit them together using basic software like the free Windows Movie Maker (https://support.microsoft.com/en-gb/help/14220/windows-movie- maker-download). The great news is that PowerPoint now lets you save your presentations as video files.

While these options all work well, by far the best option is to create videos that actually have you in them. This is far more professional, much more engaging and much easier to hype in your pre-launch phase.

To do this, you're going to need some basic equipment and you'll need to practice your presentation skills.

In terms of equipment, look for:

- *A good camera* - The Panasonic G7 is a great option that will provide good value for money and create professional looking footage. Otherwise, look for something with a screen that you can rotate to see yourself, 1080p or 4K video and 60fps frame rates.

- *Tripod* - Some kind of tripod is a necessity and the best ones come from Manofrotto. You should also consider getting a panning head, which will attach to the tripod and allow you to create panning shots of scenery and of items. This is useful when you're collecting what is known as 'b- roll'. B-roll is of course footage that you will speak over the top of.

- *Lighting* - When it comes to the quality of your footage, lighting is as or more important than your camera. Good lighting can be achieved by using a window but this leaves you very dependent on the quality of the weather. Better is to get a 'soft box', which will create a small amount of light to bask your face.

- *Backdrop* - You need a good backdrop, whether you choose to make that a room in your home, a nice park or a green screen. You can get a green screen very cheaply and this will allow you to choose any kind of backdrop you would like for your videos.

- *Music* - Hiring someone to create some music that you can use on top of your footage will help to make it much more engaging and professional-feeling.

- *Sound* - Sound quality is nearly as important as video quality and if you're using the mic built into your camera, then your creations are always going to feel amateurish. You can solve this with a hand-held recorder and a lav mic plugged into it. Alternatively, look for a Blue Yeti microphone if you are going to be sitting in one spot.

- *Editing* - You'll finally need some good editing software. Free options like MovieMaker just don't cut it at this point, so you'll want something like a

Outsourcing

As mentioned, you can create any kind of product for your launch, so the few we've touched on are only a couple of examples. But in both these examples and in many others, you will have the option to outsource the creation of your product if you prefer.

And the easiest way to do that is to head to a freelancing site like UpWork (www.upwork.com) or like freelancer.com (www.freelancer.com).

Here, you'll be able to find people who advertise their writing services or videography services at an hourly rate or per word/minute.

You can hire someone to write a 10,000 word ebook and it shouldn't cost you much more than $3OO-$500.

But a word of caution - when you hire someone to write for you, it's always important to pay a little more and get a better quality end product. There are people out there who will write your ebook for $150 but you should avoid them as the writing will likely be in broken English.

Another thing to consider, is that when you hire someone to write for you, the quality of that writing is never going to be as good as it would have been had you written it yourself. The simple fact of the matter is that other people won't care as much about your product as you do. Not only that, but they can't be expected to be true experts in the field.

When you read a bestselling physical book, this is not a book that was outsourced to a generic writer who did a bit of research and wrote up what they found. This will be a book written by someone who is deeply passionate about the subject, who has years or even *decades* of experience dealing with that subject and who has new, exciting and innovative ideas to bring to the table. This is also then what allows that book to generate the kind of buzz it does and to ultimately become a bestseller.

So, if you really want your book to become a bestseller, then you need to consider writing it yourself and writing it because you have something exciting and new to share. This will come across in your marketing and your hype too. It is *far* more effective than deciding you want to make a product in X niche and then pulling something out of the air.

CHAPTER 4

YOUR PRODUCT LAUNCH TIMEFRAME

Once you've started creating your product, you'll be able to come up with a rough timeframe for your product.

How long is it going to take you to create your product? And how long are you going to need to prepare marketing materials? The best way to decide is to start planning out your launch time-frame by thinking about all of the steps.

And it's not just a matter of knowing how long it will take you to create your product. You also need to know how long you ideally *want* it to take you. When is the best time to go live? How long do you want to let your followers wait to build the hype?

They say that comedy is all in the timing. Well, as it turns out the same is probably also true for launching a product. Or at least timing is a *big part* of what determines your eventual success or failure when trying to raise interest and money. You can have the best video and the best product in the world - but if you launch at the wrong time or don't let it run for long enough, then you might be shooting yourself in the foot.

This chapter will help you to create your crowdfunding timeline to avoid making that fatal error.

Steps to Defining Your Launch

Step 1: Preparation

Tim Ferriss, author of the *Four Hour Workweek,* talks about the importance of 'prep and pick up' if you intend to 'hack' Kickstarter (Kickstarter being the highly popular crowdfunding tool, which is essentially an advanced tool for creating a successful product launch!). Basically, the concept is that you should do a lot of the work long before you intend to launch your project to make sure everything is ready to go at the click of a button. That means you should create your video, write press releases and create e-mail templates long before your project goes live. This way, all you have to do is to hit 'send' to maximize your marketing potential. Once you go live you'll (hopefully) be too inundated with interview requests and other marketing activities to sweat the small stuff.

What you'll also find, is that this tends to mean you end up doing more as you won't be distracted by your other commitments. And there are practical considerations here too - creating a video takes time and money and you'll need to factor that into your budget when you go live. You may find you can make your video more cheaply which will give you the option to offer more valuable perks. Setting everything up in advance is a great way to account for costs and it just means you're stacking the deck in your favour.

Do your prep and pick up now and that way, you can estimate how long the actual product creation is going to take you and you'll be ready to go live based on your own timeframe. Delaying your launch can be critically damaging to your campaign otherwise, as can launching without the requisite press-releases and other marketing materials.

Step 2: Building Buzz

Of course you're not going to wait until your project goes live before you tell anyone about it though! Magazines and websites like to be able to cover *breaking news* but it takes them time to turn a press release into a beautiful feature for their site so they need to get all the information early on.

Meanwhile, you should also start building a community around your project *before* you take it to Kickstarter or Indiegogo. Why? Because that community will serve you incredibly well when it comes to drumming up support for your project. If you create some true fans, they'll not only be almost guaranteed to back you - giving the project momentum from the word go - but will also be likely to spread the word on your behalf. Then again, you also don't want to start building buzz *too early* or you can pass your peak and people will end up losing interest. Start making noises about a year before you go live and gradually increase the engagement as you build up to the big day.

Another benefit? People want what they can't have. If you tell them about something super exciting and then make them *wait* to hear more, their anticipation will grow to a fever pitch.

There are many ways you can do to generate buzz and build a community. Creating a 'pre-launch' site is one, building a social media following is another and crowdsourcing ideas can also be useful. If you're planning on using affiliate marketers to help you sell your product, then that is going to take some time in itself. Launching something on your own meanwhile, will of course be a lot faster and easier.

Again, you need to think about how long this is going to take. How long do you need to build that kind of buzz and excitement?

And partly this will depend as well on your existing engagement and following. If you have a huge audience already, then it's going to be easier for you to gain the kind of following you want!

Step 3: The Announcement

So how do you go about deciding when you want to announce your upcoming launch? Like the launch itself, you want to make the maximum splash here in order to get people talking and to start out with some solid momentum.

A good start would be to take a look at your calendar. If you're looking for funding, or you're looking for pre-orders, consider that particular times of year see people become more charitable, with Christmas being an obvious example.

Of course you might be inclined to think that people would be *less* generous at a time of year when they're likely blowing huge wads of cash on Christmas presents. Then again though, if common wisdom is to be believed then we're actually more generous when we have less. So Christmas would be a pretty good time of year! Then again though, if you *were* hoping to strike when people were feeling flush, then choosing the end of the month (28th) would mean starting your project right when people have just been paid.

Holidays like Christmas, Easter, Halloween and Valentine's Day also create new marketing opportunities for you and this is something else to consider. Christmas is a time when people may be feeling fat for instance, while New Year is a great time to sell a course or self-improvement book.

Likewise, you can also jump on other big events and even the launch of other products that might lend your campaign some extra momentum. Is your product related to comic books? Then launching around the time of the next *Avengers* movie could be a wise move. Is it an iPad accessory? Then perhaps you could wait until Apple's next conference.

Step 4: The Last Minute Push

But your announcement isn't everything. And in fact the launch date itself isn't everything either. While this is an important consideration, it's *also* important to think about is when that 'home stretch' will be - which tends to be the time you'll get the most excitement behind the initial launch. On Kickstarter, the general advice is that shorter campaigns tend to actually do better by increasing the time pressure on your backers. This can work well for a marketer's product launch too and the other big advantage of a shorter pre-launch is that it will help you to avoid people losing interest. There will be a point where your product excitement reaches fever pitch and if you drag on longer than that, then people will move on to other things.

But make your campaign *too* short and you won't have enough time to build the maximum amount of excitement or buzz.

This is also important seeing as there tends to be a last minute 'push' towards the end. Your project will have more momentum at the start and again in the final days if it follows the most common trajectories. This is your second opportunity to get people excited about your idea, so make sure it comes at a good time for you and that you're ready for it.

So when picking your start date, consider the length of your campaign and when your project will *end* as well.

This is just a rough outline to help you come up with a timeline for your marketing campaign. Of course every business is different and you might have a different strategy - just make sure you're thinking carefully about the timing of each step and how you can optimize this for maximum effectiveness.

Step 5: The Length of Launch

A final consideration is the length of the launch itself. A launch doesn't take place on a single day, there will undoubtedly be a certain amount of pomp and celebration surrounding your launch that will hopefully last a little while.

This might mean that you have a launch event for example but then run a special offer for a period of time after that. You want to think a little about how long you should try and keep your buzz going and when it's time to let your product settle into a routine.

Or of course, you also have the option to make the product available only for a limited time. If your launch 'ends', then you make the entire thing into a big, excited rush and this will create much more scarcity and urgency.

So... How Long?

If you were hoping for a straightforward answer to how long your product launch should be, then you may be disappointed.

Likewise, we haven't given you a set time and date for the product either.

But consider the following:

- A bigger, more expensive product will need a long pre-launch phase than a smaller one
- You'll need time to contact the media, work with affiliates and prepare your marketing materials
- You'll need time to develop the product if it isn't already created
- You'll want time to grow your audience, unless you already have a big following
- You don't want to lose your momentum

An ideal amount of time then might be anywhere from 7 days to 2 months. Longer than that and you risk losing people, shorter than that and it might come off a little rushed and half-baked.

But note that this doesn't mean you can't start sowing the seeds of your launch even before the announcement. You can mention that 'something is coming' for example and start to generate interest that way.

CHAPTER 5

PLANNING YOUR LAUNCH

Now your product is in development we can get to the exciting part: planning the launch.

When it comes to planning your launch, you need to think about how and where you are going to announce your product, you need to think about the stages that will lead up to your product launch. You should now have a time-frame which will be informed by the things you need to do during your launch.

We're using 'prep and pick-up' remember, which means you want to work on your marketing materials *before* your announcement. So what precisely are these materials? And what are these key milestones?

Here are some to think about:

Strategies, Materials and Milestones to Prepare for Your Launch

Write a Press Release

Writing a press release and sending it out to multiple news outlets is right off the bat a great way to start generating a buzz for your product. News stories are great because they're essentially free advertising for your product, and as long as your idea is interesting/of interest to their readers, then most editors will be happy to cover you.

The best way to get coverage like this is to send your press release early to one big news source in your industry and none of the others. The reason for this is that all publications love exclusives, and by doing this you will be more likely to headline. At the same time though, once you get covered there you'll find that you start to get more coverage from the other magazines and websites that follow suit so as not to get left behind. Don't forget to contact print sources even if you're trying to promote an online product or service, these are a great way to reach a wide audience and often there is less competition here.

The other crucial thing to do, is to tell a story. This is the fundamental truth of a press release that is missed by a huge proportion of marketers and creators.

Publications, websites and writers are not interested in helping you make money. Their job is not to provide you with marketing. Their job is to provide their audience with an exciting and interesting story so that they keep coming back and keep reading. If your story is 'Man sells ebook for regular price' then you're going to get ignored. Likewise, don't clutch at straws trying to make your boring story sound original or exciting.

I used to work at a magazine and getting clearly promotional 'press releases' was one of the most frustrating things I had to deal with on a daily basis. It also made the companies responsible look very amateurish and not particularly clued in.

Find the human interest in your launch or your product. That might be your personal story (how you started your business), or it might be the controversial, novel or exciting part of your book. Again, this is why you need something that is inherently *interesting* to build buzz.

Use Crowdsourcing

Using crowdsourcing is a great way to get your product noticed and to get help in the funding or formation of ideas. With a site like Kickstarter for instance you can get funding for your project and essentially this amounts to a lot of pre-orders and a great way to test the market reception. Other companies meanwhile have used crowdsourcing for ideas and to ask their market what they want - for instance the company 'Razer' recently unveiled the design for a new gaming tablet on Facebook and opted only to make it if it received enough likes. Such stunts not only raise awareness and are undoubtedly going to be picked up by various news sources, but also give the companies involved a good indicator as to whether or not their concept has a potential audience or if they're just spinning their wheels.

Social media is a massive asset for you to use and if your audience feels as though they were involved in the creation of the end product, they're going to end up much more excited for it. This is one more reason that crowdfunding sites work so well. You could even include the names of the people who 'helped' in your 'Special Thanks' section. This will build huge amounts of brand loyalty and they may even be moved to help you promote the product as a result.

Hold a Conference or Launch Event

Holding an event is a great way to launch any new business venture. This will automatically be a glamorous and glitzy occasion which will help to build anticipation and excitement for what you're about to announce. At the same time, you can invite the press to your event and they will likely be excited to come seeing it as a great day away from the office but also a great opportunity for a story. With an event you can then get everyone into a merry mood by having the alcohol and food flow and this will make the audience of course more receptive to whatever you unveil.

Reality check though: your press conference is not likely to be anywhere near as exciting or as glamorous as those in big industries. You need to know your limitations and work with what you have. If you can't create a big event to launch your product that will get covered by big media outlets, then instead, you can launch an online event (a Webinar for example), or you could launch something small and then stream it using video streaming software. You can even just report on your launch event and show pictures and things of you and a few friends in suits. This helps to give your product more authority and prestige and makes it seem even more premium and exclusive.

Leak Information

Businesses can learn an awful lot from the marketing strategies of Hollywood when they're launching a new film franchise - small images and teaser trailers as well as 'leaked' details can be a perfect way to whet the appetite of the general public/industry and if it can get some rumors and speculation circling then this will be great for building excitement and getting people ready for what you're going to announce. We've likewise already touched on the way that Apple and other OEMs will release rumors regarding the specs and details of their new hardware prior to the official announcements. Again, anything that can get people talking is a *very* good thing.

Stage a Viral Event

If you want to draw a lot of attention to your business, then sometimes just doing something newsworthy is the easiest way, from having people in an airport sing to passengers as they arrive to filling a portion of a city with bubbles and seeing how people react. The more you can get people to cover it the better, and if it goes viral then that's even better.

Create a Brand

Creating a brand is a very important part of any marketing process. Your brand is what's going to make your product seem like more than the sum of its parts and it's what is going to bring everything together.

It's important that your website or blog has a strong brand too. This is what will allow you to build a big following of genuine fans rather than merely customers. To go back to Apple, think how important that brand loyalty is for the success of the business *and* specifically the hype and buzz they're able to generate.

But you can also have a brand for the product itself. Think of this like the difference between Microsoft and Xbox. Microsoft is one brand and Xbox is another. Imagine if they had just sold the Xbox as a gaming PC - would it have been anywhere near as successful or big?

Design a logo, build your brand and make sure you have something that people can get excited for.

Sponsorship or Influencer Marketing

Sponsoring a big event or a sports team when it's getting a lot of media focus is a great way to bring in some attention and to ride on the success of whatever the occasion or brand you are sponsoring is. Try to use this method to create positive associations as well as to get more eyes on your product.

For most online marketers though, sponsorship is going to mean working through influencer marketers. If you can get someone to talk about your book to their huge YouTube following then this can gain you an amazing amount of buzz. Why not identify some of the key influencers in your niche on YouTube or Instagram and then give them a free beta-copy of your ebook or course to get a review? Or - to go the more traditional sponsorship route - just pay for

Competitions and Giveaways

People love getting stuff for free, and the media loves reporting on these opportunities. By offering discounts and free gifts you can get a lot of attention on you when you need it and get millions of people wanting your prize and then being disappointed if they don't win. That disappointment is a good thing though because now they'll have all the more motivation to go out and buy your exciting new product the old-fashioned way!

If this isn't your first product launch, then you can give away previous products as a way to demonstrate the quality and value you're able to provide and to get people wanting more.

Beta Tests

Letting some people use something and not others is a brilliant way to increase desirability because we all want what we can't have. Make your service or product exclusive, at least to begin with, and word will rapidly spread. This works particularly well for apps and software but you can equally provide sneak peaks for books, courses and more.

Staggered Launch

Another way to generate excitement and to get people talking is to stagger your launch. For example, you could give away the first chapter of your ebook after the first week. Or you can keep your launch running long into the future by releasing limited slots or downloads every few months.

Building a Mailing List

Building your mailing list is a very important part of the process and this should happen pre-launch and even *pre-pre-launch.* We'll talk about this more in a subsequent chapter.

CHAPTER 6

CHOOSING AN AFFILIATE
MARKETING PLATFORM

One of the best ways to get a *massive* kick up the backside for your product launch though, is to find an affiliate marketing platform and then sign up. Most people reading this will already know what an affiliate marketing scheme is but for those who don't, this essentially means that you are going to be offering commission on your product. In fact, you might even offer something in the region of 70% or more - so that the marketers make more money from their sales than you do!

This seems absurd until you consider that it isn't taking away from your earnings. You are still going to be selling your own products for 100% profit and any sales you get from the affiliates will be *additional* to what you're already earning. And if you have 100 marketers, all selling hundreds of items, then this can be very profitable indeed. Thus, offering a large commission makes good sense because that way you'll be able to get as many of them on board as possible.

Now note that affiliates *love* product launches. That's because a product launch will give them the opportunity to generate maximum buzz and therefore maximum sales. This is one more reason for an affiliate marketer to run a product launch - it gives you time to get the maximum marketing force behind your product and gets more marketers interested in representing you!

To get started, you just need to find an affiliate marketing platform to work with. While there are many options, the big ones include JVZoo, ClickBank and Infusionsoft.

3 Great Affiliate Marketing Networks

ClickBank

www.clickbank.com

ClickBank is one of the oldest affiliate marketing platforms and thus has a particularly large following, tons of products to choose from and tons of marketers to help promote those products. However, it is also somewhat more old-fashioned in the way you sign up and get started and it can be a little more of a headache to get your head around versus something like JVZoo.

JVZoo

www.jvzoo.com

As that last comment suggested, JVZoo is largely our preferred option for product creators. JVZoo is a large affiliate network that has been growing in popularity thanks to its relative ease of use and its large range of products, marketers and features.

In particular, JVZoo makes it very simple for you to set-up and manage affiliates and URLs and that way streamlines the process of getting your product out there. ClickBank may give you a slightly larger audience in certain niches though, so do a little more research before you get started.

Infusionsoft

www.infusionsoft.com

Finally, InfusionSoft is a tool that you can use to not only manage your affiliate campaigns but also to use as a CRM and email autoresponder. That means you can use it to pretty much manage your entire campaign and if you're willing to put the time and work in, then there are a lot of powerful features here that can be highly useful. The downside is that it is also a lot more complicated to get started with and that's why it's not going to be the best option for those absolute beginners just starting out.

Getting Affiliates to Promote Your Launch

We're using a high commission as the best way to get as many affiliates as possible to help us promote your launch. But what else can you do?

One other must is to run a contest. This can be a cash prize or a physical prize but either way, your aim is to award the top 10 affiliates. This now gives them even more incentive to promote your product and especially in the run up to your big launch. Compared to a product with the same commission and *no* competition, yours has just become much more popular.

You can keep your marketers informed about who is winning and who is currently ahead and by creating competition like this, you'll also be encouraging those affiliates to put even more effort and work into promoting your product.

Note that you don't only have to find affiliates directly through affiliate marketing channels either. If you have created a commission system, then you can invite others to help you promote your product for a cut of the profits too. How about an influencer for example? And another tip is to include an affiliate page, where you can provide more information about your launch, including incentives, prizes, instructions on how to get the affiliate link and more. This will allow your existing affiliates to get more information but it will also help attract your fans to the fact that they could be making money by promoting a product that they are already fond of.

Another tip? Provide ready-made materials for your affiliates such as sales pages (next chapter) emails and more. This makes less work for them, thereby providing them with

CHAPTER 7

CREATING YOUR SALES PAGE

One absolute crucial element in your launch materials, is to use a 'landing page' where you direct as much traffic as possible - from your own site but also from links on other sites etc.

Here you will then do your best to convince anyone who stops by that they need to buy your book or your course or whatever it is, and that all comes down to the way you lay it out and how convincing you can be in your writing. A landing page can be a sales page but it can also work as a squeeze page. The idea behind a squeeze page is to drive people to sign up for your mailing list and this is, as we've mentioned already, one of the very most important tools for your pre-launch phase.

If you have a really great sales script on your site, and if you are getting highly targeted traffic, then there's no reason to think that you can't get 1-2% of people to buy an e-book worth

$30. If you are then paying .20 cents per visitor using an ad network, then you'll be making a tidy (and scalable) profit without having to do... well anything really.

Landing Page Design Basics

But that's all reliant on the work you put in to start with and how good you want to make your landing page. If you're going to make a good profit, then this needs to be able to convince people who land to buy or sign up for your mailing list.

Take some time and look around other landing pages selling ebooks etc. You will notice right away that many of them have a very narrow site design that forces you to scroll down the page. There's no menu and no other buttons - because of course that would enable you to navigate away, and the point of the narrow and linear page layout is that it forces you to 'commit' by scrolling. If you spend a while reading and if you scroll down the page as you go, then as a visitor you won't want to then just leave without having done anything.

The script also plays a big part here and should be designed to keep the reader moving on to the next line. Organize your copy so that it reads almost like a cliff hanger at the end of each statement and so that each sentence or two begins a new line. This will suck the reader in and cause them to scroll down the page and before they know it, they'll be moving through the content at a rapid pace.

Using a narrative structure is also important here. People love reading stories and if you talk about your rags-to-riches story, or the way you added 10lbs of muscle in 3 months, the people are going to feel emotionally invested. Emotion is *important* here and it is this hook that will sell your product. Remember what we mentioned earlier: you can use the 'value proposition' and get your visitor to really imagine the future that your product is going to afford them. Likewise, talk about the desirability of your product - remember those words like 'feel', 'imagine' and 'touch'.

You should litter your 'buy' button then throughout the page so that people can click it at any point, and you need to appeal to the emotions of the person buying. Note that most purchases are not logical or sensible (except maybe a new toothbrush) but rather are emotional and impulsive. Another type of emotion then is to create a sense of needing to buy right away - you want to avoid the visitor going away to 'think about it', as when they come back, they'll be less likely to want to buy. To do this you need to create a feeling of panic and urgency by stating that there is a time limit on their opportunity to buy, or on your special offer. This also has the effect of creating 'scarcity', it makes the product seem more desirable as fewer people have it and it makes your buyers feel like they're a part of some exciting underground movement as a result!

Finally, consider making your buttons red if you want to raise the heartrate slightly more. This has been shown to be effective in studies: the colors red and orange hasten decisions and make us more likely to buy!

Some Tools for Your Sales Page

One of the other big things to keep in mind when getting people to sign up for your mailing list or to buy your products, is that they need to feel secure in the knowledge that your checkout system will work, that you'll be good to your word and that they'll receive the item as they should and not be risking a security leak.

In other words, you need trust and that means your site needs to look as professional as possible. To help with this, consider using a tool like OptimizePress (https://www.optimizepress.com/), which is designed specifically for creating highly converting sales pages.

Set up your payment gateway with PayPal (www.paypal.com) and use an autoresponder like MailChimp (www.mailchimp.com), Aweber (www.aweber.com) or GetResponse (www.getresponse.com) to handle collecting and sending your emails.

CHAPTER 8

MANAGING THE PRE-LAUNCH PHASE

You know all the steps and all the materials you need, now all that is left to do is to manage your pre-launch phase and to build the excitement.

Something to keep in mind during this process is **AIDA**. This stands for:

> ➤ **A**wareness

> ➤ **I**nterest

> ➤ **D**esire

> ➤ **A**ction

In other words, you start by making sure your audience is aware of your new product launch, then you follow up by getting them at least somewhat interested in it. Then you get them to really *want* the item you're planning on launching and finally, you give them the option to take action - which will be the launch date.

Start by releasing your press releases to the biggest channels if you think there is a chance they'll cover your story. You're doing this early in order to give them time to get the exclusive without hampering your own marketing options (Prior to this, I like to give a little tease by telling the mailing list audience that something 'very exciting is coming'.)

From there, you can then officially announce the news through your own channels. Likewise, reach out through your social media and get all your contacts and connections to do the same thing.

It's at this point that you need to make sure that you have a landing page ready to push your mailing list. This can be built using the tips we covered in the last chapter and it's also a great idea to include a countdown timer that will let people literally watch the time tick down to your product launch.

Normally, when you use a squeeze page to push an opt-in form, you'll use some kind of incentive like an ebook. Your aim here is to make the product launch itself the opt-in - you need to make the mystery product sound so exciting that people will want to sign up for the mailing list *just* to get access to it when it

70

comes out (you could also offer money off). This is a brilliant strategy because it means people will actively read your email correspondence and they're actually *happy* for you to use marketing talk and sales techniques!

And it *only* works with a forthcoming product - just one more example of how much easier it is to build excitement for a product!

From here, you can release more and more tidbits of information to keep your engagement high and to keep people thinking about your upcoming launch. Don't allow too much time to pass between products and try to gradually increase your frequency as you approach the big day.

Make sure to give away plenty of free content and to engage with your audience. Demonstrate your value as much as you can by uploading more blog posts and free ebooks and by plugging your upcoming product in the meantime.

Remember to get influencers in your niche involved and to run those beta tests. Let people feel like a part of the event and create a feeling of community and exclusivity around it.

You can also create a video preview of your product, run an event and try to get social media coverage, conduct interviews etc.

Meanwhile, try and start recruiting your affiliates. Have a separate opt-in for affiliates and make sure that your marketers have all the materials you've prepared for them ready for the launch.

CHAPTER 9

THE LAUNCH PHASE

Make sure you leave yourself time to test your sales funnel and to ensure that all your affiliate links, downloads and materials work and load properly.

Gradually, that clock will tick down and eventually your product will be ready to go live. Make sure that you email your audience once more and let them know you're going live in 1 hour. Likewise, make sure that your affiliates know when it is time to start really pushing the product.

And with that, you're going to see those orders start flooding in!

This can be a very nerve-wracking moment as a creator after so much build-up and excitement. It's easy to have inflated expectations and to hope to see thousands of sales overnight. My advice is not to keep checking the sales or it can drive you mad!

The Last Push

As we've discussed, it's a good idea to have a 'launch window' which will either mean you have a limited-time special offer, or that you have a limited availability for your product generally. Either way, this works well if you limit it to around 7 days and that gives your affiliates the perfect amount of time to really push your product and for your customers to get buying.

During this period, try to maintain the buzz by emailing your audience to let them know that the product is still live and that time is running out, and your affiliates to keep them updated about the leaderboards. As time starts running out, take advantage to remind everyone how long they have and to point out that this is their *last chance*.

If you're using a sales page, then you can also use this opportunity to run a PPC campaign on Facebook Ads or Google AdWords. This will drive even more people to your page where they can conceivably convert directly if they are well-targeted. Having a fixed launch period will help you to know precisely how much you're able to budget on these ads too.

You can also continue to promote your product in other ways - keep publishing new, free content to your site (now would be a perfect time to create a series that you expect to make a big splash) and keep inviting influencers to take part. In other words, don't 'set it and forget it' but instead, keep on pushing and have events, contests and more planned to try and stoke the fires.

And the closer you get to the end, the bigger that push should become.

Again, you should have used the 'prep and pick-up' technique, meaning that all the materials you'll need should be ready to go for you to simply click 'send' on.

CHAPTER 10

POST-LAUNCH AND CONCLUSIONS

After the 7-day window is over, you can finally relax and start to calm down again. The rush is over and all that build up will hopefully have proven worth it. At this point, you'll either end your special offer and let the sales continue to trickle in, or you'll have cancelled the product altogether.

So, what now?

One thing to consider before you say goodbye to your launch, is to run a second chance saloon. During the launch, you will have let your followers know that they only have so long to complete a purchase and to get involved in what will seem like a massive, exciting event.

But some people will miss out on the opportunity. Either they weren't convinced at the time, they didn't have the available funds, or perhaps they were away. Maybe they were really busy or perhaps they missed the emails!

This is why it's a great idea to run a 'second chance saloon'. In other words, give your followers one last opportunity to buy your product/to get it at the discount price. This can work really well, as long as you leave it the right amount of time - long enough to let people think you're serious but not so long that they forget and move on to other things.

Another job for your post-launch is of course to take care of your buyers and your affiliates. This is really important because a bad product or poor after-sale-care is going to hurt your brand and prevent successful launches in future. The ideal scenario is that everyone who has bought from you now should be ready and willing to go for the next product you launch. Thus, you need to make sure they have a fantastic experience and that they'll want to do business with you again. This way, each launch will build on the last and will be bigger and more successful than the one before it!

Don't forget to thank your affiliates too, to dish out the contest rewards and to make sure they also want to work with you next time.

Product Launch: The Sequel

Because there will be a next time. Not too soon, but after you've let things die down a bit you can start thinking about how to follow this launch up with the next.

It's very important during your product launch to track all metrics and any signs of success or failure. You should know exactly how many items you sold, where your biggest sources of converting traffic were etc. This will let you perform a debriefing that you can then use to inform and improve your next launches.

CONCLUSIONS

What you'll find is that the entire thing can be quite a rush. An exciting rush but a tiring and stressful one too! This is why it's so important that you plan everything in advance and prepare all those materials so that they're ready to go when you launch. You want to lay out each step as much as possible so that all you have to do is click 'publish', 'send' and 'post' when the time comes.

Planning your launch in this way will give you a much greater impact and truly drive an unstoppable wave of sales that can give your product a much needed boost when it needs it most - but of course it also means that your sales are likely to drop for a while in between.

Hopefully, by using all of the tips and advice in this book, you will now know precisely how to run a successful product launch from the ideation, to the creation, to recruitment and building buzz. Employ this correctly and you should find it entirely changes the game and drives the kind of traffic that you could only dream about before.

But the very most important thing? To create a product that people will genuinely get passionate and excited for. Make something that is newsworthy and that people can *get* hyped about. Your passion will come across and the excitement of your audience will grow tenfold as a result.

And that is how you will avoid a failure to launch...

IMPORTANT: To help you further take action, print out a copy of the *Checklist* and *Mindmap* I provided. You'll also find a Resource Cheat Sheet with valuable sites, posts and articles that I recommend you go through.

CPSIA information can be obtained
at www.ICGtesting.com
Printed in the USA
LVHW080209290323
742929LV00018B/278